The Storm That Tames Us

The Storm
That Tames Us

Renée Gregorio

LA ALAMEDA PRESS :: ALBUQUERQUE

For editorial help in the making of this book, I want to thank Marsha Skinner, John Brandi, Joan Logghe and Jeff Schneider for their insights, suggestions and understanding, all which made a difference; thanks to Carla Prando for her intense reading of and comments on "Pulling Vinca"; and thanks to Jeff Bryan for his editing suggestions to an earlier version of the manuscript. For introducing me to the idea of *hara* or center, and for being my teacher in that arena of the dojo, I thank Takashi Tokunaga.

Thanks to the editors of the following publications
where some of these poems first appeared:
This Harsh Desire for Other (TAOS REVIEW, *No. 4, 1991*)
The Remedy (THE ELEVENTH MUSE, *Vol 11, No 2, Winter 1993*)
Two Floating Shapes (NEXUS, *Fall 1997, Vol 33*)
The Other Voices (HEAVEN BONE, *Issue Eleven, 1994*)
Moving to Light (SALUDOS! *Pennywhistle Press, 1995*)
Solitude Dinner (WRITTEN WITH A SPOON, *Sherman-Asher, 1995*)
Gladiola, The Storm That Tames Us (FRANK, *1998*)
Embracing the Ordinary (PRACTICE OF PEACE, *Sherman-Asher, 1998*)
Reincarnate *(*VEHICLE, *1998)*
toasted hazelnuts (AMERICAN TANKA, *1998*)
Islands of Contained Light, Raking the Wild, The Painted and
the Real, The Beginning Island (SANTA FE POETRY BROADSIDE, *1998*)
Triangle of Light *(*FISHDRUM, *1999)*
I Tasted Him... (TUNDRA, *1999*).

Cover painting: Marsha Skinner
"Untitled" *oil on canvas*

ISBN: 1-888809-16-7
Library of Congress #: 99-71683

La Alameda Press
9636 Guadalupe Trail NW
Albuquerque, New Mexico 87114

to John Brandi,
husband and comrade

Contents

Move like a beam of light:
Fly like lightning,
Strike like thunder,
Whirl in circles around
A stable center.

Morihei Ueshiba
the founder of Aikido

Moving to Light

He threw me once.
That's all it took.
Just the clean sweep
of his foot along the mat
and I was done for—tumbled and caught
by rushing gust of wind.
My body flew up
then down fast,
to the coin's edge
between pain and pleasure,
where there's only
the throb of the *yes* of the moment.

Then I knew the cleanliness
of energy coming from all of him,
knew what it meant to be at the rope's
middle, that still and centered point
between opposing forces tugging for position.

Even childhood was never so right,
all that holding back, afraid of speech that would reveal
me, always a veil over my eyes and face like an ancient bride.
The veil, which held me away from the scent
of the likes of him, even from myself.

When he threw me there was no thought before or after.
He woke me from dreaming,
maybe a lifetime of it, and when I turn in that direction,
there is light coming up over a mountain—

it is no less than the light of a full moon
in this star-ridden desert sky. His sky has stars in it, too.
I saw them begin to reveal themselves,
only a few scattered in that once-fogged dark.

Only a few,
but I remember their brilliance as I remember him later pushing me
back onto the table, my silk under his thick hands,
and to me it seemed the whole audience must have turned toward us—
there was so much light.

This Harsh Desire for Other

He draws me in like the mountains
seem to draw the rain down, furtive
pulling, the way hunger moves
grumbling in the early stages,
asking all,
open-mouthed, anxious.

I've driven down roads with no streetlights,
adrift in huge fields, the horizon unseen
or unreachable. I've felt hunted, running fast,
always something tight to my back.
I'm not afraid anymore.
I want to shake at the root.

I do not say *I love you* on abandoned benches
in deserted parks. I say it on the subway,
noise and people crowding our bodies, the more
inapt the place, the better. I will say it
everywhere. I don't need him here. I conjure him
sharp as the nettle's quick, reverberating sting.

I am at home in silence,
though it can consume like waves
in the Atlantic, so vast
they obliterate breath. I live in awe
of that which is split when once it was whole,
like the Rio Grande gorge divides
the earth's plates into uncrossable chasm.
I have been the stone in the river

a man stepped on to get across.
I've followed the arc of desire far out
into a wild universe. I came to men's voices
with the heart of a little girl.
Does monogamy mean I will never be touched
by another man under the moon's rising light?
I stare at a photograph where a thousand birds
take flight in the space above a woman's head.

I touch his arms, his chest,
I press my hands into flesh
to make him mine, take him into me,
to let all the others drop away.
We broadcast years of information
in a single breath, the air wiser for it.
I didn't know I loved the sound
of two rivers coming together,
or entering someone else's sadness
like a drumbeat, feeling it in the center
of the heart, the hungry self
salivating, this harsh desire for *other*.

Love's a Shock

It is an odd quality of yearning one finds
looking up again at the stars as if
there is something to be learned from them—
distance and light, patterns shifting and unknown—
yet I keep seeing the big and little dippers,
shapes recognized even in childhood.

It is the same quality looking out from shoreline
to sea, waves curving up over each toe,
numbing the edge of skin then rushing
back out again as if they had somewhere important to be.
It is the rushing I'm tempted to follow, that sense
of entering something broad, deep, shifting.

It's true that love is a shock—
and the more entire, the more shocking.
Yet here, there's nothing to be changed, only lives
to be moved through and I am on the edge of loving
you as if on the edge of a pool contemplating
the sleek water's surface and what's required

to break through. Yes, I know how dangerous
that dive can be: at ten I scraped my front tooth
on the pool's bottom at the YWCA and my mother's words:
the awful thing is, it will always be that way, it's permanent.
I felt such shame at having gone too far, too deep, at knowing
I dove in unconsciously, then lost part of myself.
Here, I turn toward you all night long.
All the men I've ever lost I find again in you.

It is the way you don't let me go that I love,
and then the way you do. I go back to all the forgotten
selves, your hands reach out to meet mine in the night
and there are words you say that I know in my body

from other languages, words that bring the heat up
out of my body and into your hands. And though I love
words as I am beginning to love you, it's the words
I want to wade through to the open and empty field
where we will simply be two individuals basking
in substance and light. I did not grow out of this soil;

I had the Atlantic for vastness, not this desert sea.
But I grow into this soil; years later I have become
bleached bone in this hot sun, the nameless river,
a dry arroyo, the tiny pool of water bubbling up out of ground
at the ditch's origin. What is source for you
is my beacon. But, they lead to the same place,

to this heart's core that grows between us as you rest
against me on the hard dirt of the *barrancas* and we look out
at the Sangres, the Truchas, Baldy Peak, all in the near distance.
We look out at once in the same direction and in the quick
flight of our days, call this home. This is the new territory
of loving, where nothing is lost or expected, everything a gift

of river and mountain, blood and bone, sweat and singing,
a gift of words exchanged, prayers recognized.
I face you and our differing heritage knowing there have been nights
I'd drive all the way to you, no matter how far.
Yes, I have loved the cold beauty of the north. Now I learn
not to believe in the sketch of promise portioned out of hunger,
but instead in the fever of what's in front of me. Every time I see you
it is the first time, every touch between us the beginning of knowing

flesh. We gather pleasures together, courting happiness
as if it's something we haven't had in a very long time.
When we walk on the earth, we become the earth and we also let it be.
When we enter water, we remember the ocean of our first birthing.

At dawn and sunset, the light shifts toward another way
of being—the first light when all is possible and the last
light, rich with seed, tenuous and glowing,
neither dark nor light, the transitory,
the unmasking, the awakening.

Triangle of Light

There is not much time.
I must tell you everything right away.
How this morning, blurry and tired, I reached
under the kitchen chair to pick up what looked like
something, yet it was simply a triangular patch of light
formed by sun and obstruction.

I come to these words
out of a floating world that's supposed to be made
only of pleasure. I am good at the momentary,
crawling into that triangle of light,
washed out by its intensity.
I hardly know you, yet last night,
driving to Albuquerque alone, my body
craved you, opened to you,
pomegranate spilling sweet seed.

That red stains all of my fingers.
It's you I want to put those fingers in,
wherever you'll let me. You are cruel
to make me burn this way, cruel as March
winds sticking it out through April,
how these nights freeze the daffodils
and the buds on the apricot tree,
how they may never recover to bear fruit.

Bloom

I have had things my way and liked it:
the day split by paper and skin,
orange poppies you pointed at
out the kitchen window cranked open
to air and the sound of chainsaw.
We let the light in.

I like the way you wash me
softly with warm water after
we make love hard, you
all the way to the end of me.
Your eyes let the light in.

Your heart is pounding,
but not with love. I would call it love
but I can hear you say *oh no*
all the way back to a childhood
and a past I know little about.

I ask you what it is you want
from me and you answer: *everything*.
So do I. Especially you backing into me
on the bed, curling into my chest, letting me
kiss your hair and hold you as if you
belonged there. It is like coming home.

I make so much of this
because there is so much to be made.
Today the light between us glares.

I bask in it like any good day of sun,
come away marked with a dark tan.
It is the way you grab my hand,

Hold it away from you,
as much as anything else that makes me
want you. It is also the way you are not
afraid to touch me through to what's behind
the muscle, what's underneath
the blood. You cure me of an old injury
with hands sharp as lightning, soft as turned earth.

You give yourself away wherever you can.
I would gather you up like a precious bouquet,
take your scent in, feed the flowers
cut from their roots till they opened,
petal by petal, in this harsher light of day.

God Went Away for the Winter, She Said

It's hard between two people.
Some days we walk the clouds of these mountains.
Others I hear only complaints, the straight
lines of will. Embracing the ordinary
is wrestling the winter-god. Note the shifting
color of your skin. What is the same
can gather strength, a rolling snowball,
can be ally, mistress, lover.
Yesterday I woke to three rainbows
on the living room floor, your chest
rising and falling under my splayed fingers.
Today you said *Look at that*, pointing
to the intricate spaces between the piled wood.
It's an accident, you said, meaning the beauty
that arrived outside our window, or
that you noticed it. I have a bar of soap
from Mexico with a man and woman kissing.
My friend's gift. *This brings the man you want
to you*, she said. On the wall there's a photo
of you and me kissing, years ago now, on a patio
in Santa Fe. That alchemy once came to us, will again.
It's hard between two people. In December I wrote:
*Dearest love. This is the world we've always wanted,
our breath rising and falling like one hundred magpies
under the dying lilac bush. The sun is hiding.
We are our own best kindling.*

The Long Hill of Garrapata

1

I always had to climb the long hill of Garrapata to get back to you,
knew the way my aging car would slow for its incline,
knew what the house would smell like when I arrived, its mixture
of wood-smoke and eucalyptus leaf browning on top of the Ashley
and your skin with its paint and sweat and your grey hair caught
under the rim of your Stetson. You'd tell me: *I heard you coming
from the bottom of the mountain.* We would laugh, knowing
how much we each listened for the sound of the other.
You placed the striped rock from the mesa on a post outside
the front door, named it my homing rock. It worked.

2

Many years ago, my grandmother called me *precious.*
I might have been five, looking up at her through clasped
hands, wondering what the word meant. Now I know
the innocence that can only exist before there's a word for it,
that I trusted her utterly to take me down the street to the square
and back home again safely, that there was such a thing as safety
and that I owned it. Death changes all that. Before the word
for death, just the sense of looking out on an empty,
surging sea. The sound of death makes me want
someone's hand to hold, someone who can take me safely home.

3

Here I am, on the face of the earth without you.
If I dig in the vacant lot that is my garden, I think of your body,
now turned to ashes, feeding the earth that was once our home.
If the wind is strong, I imagine you going places, as you used to dance
with your feet planted and your arms swirling like propellers—
the violent weather becomes you. When the hummingbirds feed
outside my bedroom window, you must want to tell me something
crucial, so I listen. I have planted you a thousand times since your death,
as if through digging, another one like you might find a way into me.

4

I map this sudden territory of dark the dead occupy,
the other side we know little about, yet now I want to know
what happens in death because you are there and I want to know you,
as I always have. Williams said: *Death / is not the end of it.*
I believe him as I used to believe you when you told me
you loved me, when you said you couldn't go on.

5

It is quieter here now. On the phone wire,
it is never your voice. We are all growing older
without you. Your death made your daughters
more beautiful. I am watching them, thinking of you.
They carry your weight, made of both thunder and water.
I call them precious. The homing rock takes me to the *barrio*.
You are my angel. I hear you coming from the back
side of the mountain. There are times you are so noisy
I know death is not where you end.

Reincarnate

we could be trees grown next to each other
only I'd have to be quiet sometimes, you said,
and I said you'd be one of those trees that never stop
swaying, and we could be the harsh resonant beat of drum,
skin stretched taut and the stick   we could be
coho salmon in Eagle Nest Lake fished for
through 20-inch-thick ice   we could be the lake itself
we could be the smoke in the air between us
in the Ford pickup   we could be the way the road winds
we could be etched fish and bird in stone
we could be the parallel lines
on the highway   we could be the singing bowl
and the wood that elicits its sound   we could be hungry,
on the streets, our palms up   we could be snakes
in desert grass, the dust from stars, the tail of a comet,
the mouse under the bed, the road on a map,
just hands, just mouths, just eyes   we could be
manatees, crows, swallowtail butterflies, the new moon,
or blood and bones again, searching
the root of the other
we could be.

Five Seasons

I went to visit
a man who drew a map
with red pen, white paper,
and tore the piece at odd angles,
fingers rich with waiting.

All night the skin warms.
All day the river freezes—
lovemaking at dawn.

I tasted him
and he tasted good, like the sea,
a wanting
made of salt and wind,
and just as vast.

Run three miles, think of
past four lovers, the in-
significance of numbers.

one by one
she touches each shirt's fibers,
arranges them
in his rented closet—
an act more intimate than lovemaking.

Islands of Contained Light

For years I've searched men's songs,
pulled them out like fish out of a dark river,
eaten them whole, swallowing my father's absence.
I used to want to change lives,
even if that meant destruction.
But it was never home, how could it be?
Home was in my head, a kernel of longing.

I barely know that other woman now,
the one who used feeling as drug.
Everything slowed down so I could see
each tendril of light. I followed the path
that's left when water leaves the riverbed,
searching one stone with a bloodline
I could hold in my hands.

Memory enters blood.
So many I have left
to their own lives, islands
containing their own light now.
I am left here
to go down into that underground territory,
the one I stand in with my rake.
I write against the door's banging, every storm
reveals tentacles of light
streaming down into the dark
breath of roots.

The Breath Inside the Breath

1

This is the season of falling away,
falling back. I hear it in the leaves,
a sound like dying.

This season of brilliant color
muted by cold. I watch as the wind
tears the leaves from their branches.

It is beyond the time I brought dark
into light with hands surrounding me
with their own sort of breath

as if I were an instrument music
could rise up from. No, these days
I read Kabir asking his student:

Tell me, what is God?
And the answer: *He is the breath*
inside the breath.

2

I am walking down the road to a stream,
holding nothing in my hands, jumping over sand
to reach a tiny island where water flows

on both sides of me. Here I find comfort;
water diverges directly in front
of my face. I can hear it and touch it—

its sound is alive in me.
At this place I find the strength to kneel,
fill my hands with water, and drink.

I come here for refuge and re-claiming what should never
have been lost, this stretch of *barrancas* I climb
to the top of, find my feet planted

on an earth I never knew anything about.
At the summit I find a worn, ancient footpath
and travel on.

Existential Saturday

Tonight, there's doubt in the sound
of my own breath, in the skin-border,
the voice-cry, the sudden desire my breasts
have for hands—anonymous, figurative as shadow-play.
If no one's watching, do I exist?

When I'm alone on a Saturday night,
I begin to imagine a time not far from now, children
wrapping their bodies around mine, a riper life.
Yet that abstraction, desire, rises up again,
spreads itself thin across the North American continent.
There are so many men I'd follow to the ends of the earth,
and none I have. I eat food I've grown
in a shared garden that went unweeded.
I eat to fortify what's otherwise
ethereal. To claim my body as real.

Last night, I dreamt of four lions, all of them
my friends. No one's here but me to speculate
the meaning of these things.
Everyone fails me.
I'm motherless, fatherless, homeless, causeless,
featureless as blinding snow, fluid as a fast-
running acequia, liquid and untouchable as mercury.

The Angel Tells Me

learn to listen with your whole body
she tells me

and I say I want to be with him
till my bones ache

she says I think a certain amount of praying
will be necessary

and I say I want to cut through this
like breaking a glass bottle over flagstone

and she says be raw
in your emotions

and I say I long to be
living in danger

and she says there is another territory
between the wild and the rational—live there

so I say who has the key?
is it the car mechanic?

—my hands gripped tight around his thick waist
loving that wiry territory under the hood?

and she says you know
where your lips are

and I say I am ready
to burrow in

and she says don't fall over into it
like shouting down a well

and I say already there are too many
echoes in me

and she says lay a tribute
to what's broken

and I say I will burn candles
next to the shards of glass

and she says explore the dimensions
of your clashing desires

and I say I am afraid
to drive through blinding snow

and she says the musicality of chance
and I say this beginning breaks over me

and she says dive fully
under the harsh surface of water

and I say I have been
in shadow too long

and she says I am your intimate witness
and I say you are the unsounded voice in my head.

The Remedy

So, I'm at Cid's Market,
the fancy natural foods store in Taos,
reading the bottles' labels, my eyes
suddenly drawn to "Depression Complex".
Down the homeopathic list of states
of mind this little bottle might cure are
depression, grief, anxiety, and those only the beginning.
I am amazed there's a bottle
that claims to cure grief!
Suddenly, I'm embarrassed,
holding onto this cure
with a little too much interest,
and there are people walking by me now.
If they see me, they'll know I'm depressed.
I quickly return Depression Complex to its little shelf
next to the echinacea, which I purchase.
Immune system deficiency is not embarrassing to me,
though I do get too many sore throats.
Now I listen to Tracy Chapman's first tape,
the one in which she's always saying *I'm sorry, I love you.*
I begin to cry. Nothing will cure this,
except really sobbing, which I'm not prepared to do,
having done it twice today already. So I sing.
And the words enter me, her words, not my own,
but they become my own, I make them into my own song,
which is part banshee, but keener, more raucous.

Dog Bite

He just came at me, growling and ridiculous.
I turned and yelled at him loudly
but by then the blood was already
rising up to the surface of skin,
making its mark.

I didn't like looking at my thigh's
darkening, then yellowing,
yet it made me feel I'd been somewhere
difficult   and back again.

The pride I used to feel at confessing
nonexistent sins to the parish priest
came back   and the silly penance
for having done nothing wrong at all
except lying about sinning so I'd have something
to say to him in the dark box of the confessional.

Then one day I looked at my thigh
and suddenly the bruise had gone.
The healing astonished me
as much as the discoloration had
and I felt something happened
without my noticing or permission.

What a world! I thought,
slowly learning to wake up.

Embracing the Ordinary

Annie Dillard aimed for the block,
splitting wood. That aiming beyond what's right
in front of you to get through it. I've decided
I must stare so hard at the wood I'm splitting

That it disappears.
Annie aims for the block, I enter oblivion, seeing
the trees and the forest all at once. It's pure,
hearing the snap in my body, where things can still split open.

The world rushes in then, chainsaws and trees falling to earth.
We make it familiar by attempting to name each sound.
But it's the books I never want to leave behind,
their spines and odd titles, other people's stories

Drawing me in, these precious
other lives. I thought of wanting to know
the names of trees. That's all. Like that one
that looks like a willow, its branches aflame at the top.

Its leaves are fed from above, its roots
from below. Dirt clinging, they keep burrowing
down, down. It is that way with trees, whatever
they're called. They need to be fed.

Let's shed what doesn't serve anymore: the rotting bark.
Take the light in. Drink the water.

Two Floating Shapes

I am not in the shadow at my father's side.
I am of the noon, the long dark one that stretches
out from him directly. When he turns I am
never there because I am also turning.

I will keep turning towards the face of his absence.
It is a burning log I watch till there's nothing
but ash and smoldering, the heat of it
drifting upwards.

When my father and I finally met,
I recognized the joining of two floating shapes,
the soldering of a deep rift.
I remember it as two shapes suddenly fitting.

I have been far out of body
in that odd place of tears, the place that knows things
before they happen, the place I have and am nothing.
I have felt the loss of the child,
the blood rushing out of me.
The loss of that father.

Digging at the river of sleep,
I know the invisibility of roots
and how we want to grasp them anyway
in our bare hands. I have seen scars
on the trunks of aspens where strangers
carved the design of their initials.
The bark of those trees swelled like skin does,
in that exact position of healing.

Aiki

This is the beginning place, the place the cup
gets emptied and I am bare
as blank page,
layers peeled away,
onion finding its fleshy center.
It could make me cry here, such openings
finding voice, finding spirit underneath spirit.
Or I could laugh here over something partially
obscene, partially hidden. I could laugh here
at the difference between *erratic* and *erotic*,
at the ways I'm thrown. Or my head could get turned
in several directions at once, showing the way I hold on too tightly,
the way one energy can shut me down, shut me up,
while another makes me want to sing loudly and off-key.
This is the place body finds her voice—
as good as coffee ice cream and bumper cars,
kid at a carnival,
as ready as a fresh wound
for new skin to emerge.

The Other Voices

I have motions of my own among the fixed stars—
planet, wanderer. The Hopi say air links
our breathing. I saw the great star on West Mesa.
That's why I landed here into this settled life,
this balancing. The Eskimos say the heart
of a young girl became the shaman's first drum.
Her muscle drawn tight to make that deep
drumbeat, to help them enter magic.

Did they take her life for that heart?
Was it still beating when they tore it apart,
stretched it for their instrument's sake?

I have motions of my own among the fixed stars—
planet, wanderer. That other world of dreaming,
of shining in the dark, those other senses
the blind know more about than us.
Someday it'll be like running down a hill—
running, but not away. I enter the spirit
in the psyche to be other, to be whole.
I am going beyond the last fence.

Phases of Moonlight

Don't mistake pointing
at the moon for the moon itself,
the politician said.

Like diving into a dark pond:
entering, entering
the movement
of one's life—
barely comprehending it.

On the senator's desk—
they're real because they're dying—
vase full of red tulips.

Moonlight on fields,
smooth stone from riverbed,
geese squawking overhead—
his eyes before and after
they were bloodshot.

clutching the bamboo
unafraid of being watched—
downy woodpecker

His studio of death:
wooden boats he carved by hand,
grim reapers he painted—
holding the seeds of his dying
in the palms of both his hands.

I hold strong coffee,
the morning soft with longing,
outside, spring snow.

the datura
for all its whiteness, blossoms
in the dark
fragrance overpowering,
one time only, even the moonlight

Da Molto Lontano

Far away, as in an echo,
water flows under lifted barricades,
makes its rough way down mountains
into tanks, stock ponds, gardens.

Thunder is a sound that seems to come
from very far away, a rumbling that fills
the body from the gut, outward, like hunger.
One peers into sky at the sound, as if it could be seen.

We all have sounds at the root of us,
sounds our bodies know and move towards,
and we seek to match those inward sounds
with something loud in the outside world. Echoes
that run in us, like the sound of someone walking away.

In Palenque, we climbed sixty-nine steep, stone
steps to reach the top of the Temple of Inscriptions.
Da molto lontano, we heard the scratching of the Mayans,
their slabs of hieroglyphics, stories
we must read backwards. We stood
surrounded by pages of stone, reading back
into their lives, the jungle dense,
moist and dark around us.

I didn't know then about all the felled mahogany, the selling
of their way of life, the felled dreams of the Mayans,
of my own ancestors, remembering my grandfather's illusions
as he neared death, his own failing powers.

I want to be used like a rake or a hoe, as Rilke did,
as all people who live *da molto lontano*, stretching the mind
and the body to meet the faraway sounds. It's all a matter of daring,
throwing off the garb of the spectator, standing ready,

Melding all the disparate thoughts
into a whole idea that moves, deepens and widens
as it goes, the same as the water that falls down the mountains,
the same as the Rio Grande, making deep chasms in the earth,
bringing the faraway sound into our bodies, breathing it at last.

Da molto lontano:
make the music sound
as if it's coming
from very far away.

Raking the Wild

I rake raw dirt,
spread seed as if it mattered
that things be given the chance to grow.
This wilderness made
of earth hard from neglect.
What does manage to grow has come
randomly and with abandon—
mostly weeds and sprigs from the Chinese elm
that take tenacious hold in
the soil of the old riverbed.

The only thing to do is begin.
Rake till the soil has breath.
Plant seeds of wildflowers
in this yard defined by chaos,
wanting to believe
they will take root and grow.

This neighborhood belongs to anyone who dares—
high-heeled shoe on bare concrete,
drains where water goes all the way to the river,
families who've lived here through grandchildren—

Barelas, where sun sets under birdsong and clammer.
An old woman walks by with her hair braided tightly
to her head, holding the hands of two dark-skinned boys.
I watch from the organic fortress that is my house,
clear burlap bags, Burger King wrappers, Styrofoam cups
from the empty lot of my yard.

An old man in a grey suit and felt hat
walks through the abandoned alley on his way to church,
bows his head in greeting,
his elegance spilling into this seasoned air.

Solitude Dinner

Day after day, I learn to be grateful.
It's a feast no matter what's on the platter—
I bow to the green beans and the roasted red
peppers, I bow to the pasta for being there
all my life, hear my grandmother say *no, it's macaroni.*
No one says that word anymore; the yuppies have taken the word
from my Italian ancestors, made it their own.
I am not a yuppie. I live in the *barrio* where no one's Italian,
no one's a woman alone.

Behind these walls, I eat the dinner of solitude.
It is a quiet meal, with candles and sometimes flowers
freshly cut from my garden. It is a meal that I need both hands
to eat, forking the macaroni with one and sopping up oil
with bread in the other. It is a meal of invention.
Last night Hugh Grant came—it was before he got caught
in a car with a prostitute and hauled off for being lewd.
I tell you, it's probably because I refused to sleep with him.

He didn't seem particularly miffed at the time; of course
the food was excellent and he liked dripping the olive
oil into his opened mouth from the heel end of the Italian loaf—
those Brits! He also ate an abnormal amount of the wrinkled
Sicilian olives I love best. Maybe that did it. At any rate, he left
smiling. What a pity to read of him in the news today.
What a drag to be famous!

I like eating alone. But sometimes Galway Kinnell comes.
He always wants oatmeal.

And then there's the visits with Adrienne Rich and sometimes
Ted Hughes and if I'm lucky Sylvia Plath shows just before Ted leaves,
and then there's the more familiar who visit: John, Joan, Miriam, Jeff,
Sawnie, Jimmy, Jaime, Ken, Peter, Bill, Ava and that guy
I met in a workshop once whose name I forget.

But sometimes no one comes at all. It's simply me and my macaroni
and the air hot with solstice and Fourth of July explosions,
the neighborhood kids all riding their bikes down the street,
shouting and calling each other's names.
The dogs keep barking as the street darkens and I finish my meal.

It is during these solitude feasts that I can hear
the voices of past dinners most clearly. All the way back
to childhood when the meals were ready when we got home
and we were sure of our places at the table. All the way back

To each dining experience with each mate
of the evening, remembering in particular the meals
when the food was incidental and what mattered was only Forster's
Only connect.
When the company was right we did it over greasy burgers,
fries and dark beer. The arrangement on the plate wasn't crucial.

In grateful solitude, all lives in what feeds us.

Resolution

This is the woman who splits wood, builds fire
This is the woman who has teddy bears, wants grandchildren
This is the woman turning ninety in a big brick house on a hill
This is the woman writing poems in the south about a child being born
This is the woman in the *barrio* holding her baby in one arm
                                        and a paperback in the other
This is the woman planting bulbs, planting trees, turning soil
This is the woman who desires to be childless,
                                who makes jewelry of hands and silver
This is the woman who heals the bodies of children
This is the woman who has a black belt in Aikido, a master of blending
This is the woman shuffling down Fourth Street
                        with her crazy stories and her jacket open
This is the woman with the Ph.D. living on Harlem's edge,
                                                spirited at 65
This is the woman who didn't want the divorce, who lives in a studio
This is the woman whose husband wanders and she knows it
                                                but is silent
This is the woman who's running, who's hunted,
                                who's driven, who's restless
This is the woman too much in love with loving as if it were elixir
                                                as if it were god
This is the woman whose father died too young
This is the woman who's too young for her father to die
This is the woman who learns how to have men as friends
                        before, after and whether they're lovers
This is the woman reading a book about a woman who's oppressed
                                                by poverty by shame
This is the woman whose father raped her

This is the woman who owns her own home, loves solitude
This is the woman who teaches Russian immigrants
                                        how to speak English
This is the woman from Brooklyn who makes pizza
                            with onions and the hearts of artichokes
This is the woman who writes novels, has two daughters,
                                        lives by the bay
This is the woman who lifts weights, runs city streets
This is the woman who built her own home, loves a man
                    she wasn't supposed to, has a three-legged dog
This is the woman who thinks she wants too much from her husband
This is the woman who loves a man twenty years younger,
                goes to rock concerts, makes a mean gin and tonic
This is the woman who opened a video store
                                    in downtown Albuquerque
This is the woman who writes poems in the dry heat and cold
                                        of La Puebla
This is the woman nearing forty who wants to be a mother
This is the woman not yet a woman who would be her child
These are the women who are dying
These are the women who are living
These are the women who are silent
These are the women who are speaking
These are the women we must be.

Crazy Priscilla's Lover

He beats me up, she said,
her face crooked as a stroke victim,
and maybe she was.

He sits around drinking all day,
and then he hits me
because he says I don't clean the house.

Priscilla shuffles down Santa Fe Avenue
toward Fourth Street, her pants baggy,
jacket open. She always stops to talk.

God bless you, she says,
my name is Priscilla,
I am your neighbor.

Each time she goes by
she introduces herself
as if it's the first time

And maybe it is.

Crazy Priscilla Goes To Confession

Bless me father, she says,
for I have sinned.
I yelled at my man because
he's not good to me.

I spent all our money
buying his beer; I can't say no
to him, even though drink makes him mean.

Some days I am mad all day long.
Sometimes people ignore me and I wish bad things on them.
Sometimes I would like to be another person.

Is that bad, father, not to like yourself?
Is it bad not to want to go home again?
Is it bad to wish your man would just die?

Yes, I have sinned if these are sins.
I am so sorry. God bless you, father.
You are such a good man.

Crazy Priscilla, Clairvoyant

She said the president announced
there must be only one dog per person.
She said she has a .38 at her house
and the right to kill all extra dogs
at each household in the neighborhood.

Every time I'm out of doors, I see her.
This means she must walk by many times a day.
I'm tilling the soil, feeding the flowers.
She says: *Oh! So pretty! You're so good;
You make it beautiful here.*

When I'm home with my lover and we sit
on the front steps, Priscilla always appears.
At just the right moment, she asks us:
Do you have any children?
How does she know we have been talking
of this for weeks now—it'll probably split us up.

Well, you will, she says. *Don't worry! You will!
They will be beautiful!* And she carries herself away from us
counting her spare change out loud, walking toward
the Arrow Market, to spend it all in one place.

Crazy Priscilla Talks Directly To God

Could you make everything right again?
Could you please make sure that all those people
who belong to each other find each other,
even if they already have and just need to be reminded?
And would you make sure that the cops in Barelas
leave me alone next time when the gunshots end
and I'm the only one left wandering the streets? I don't own a gun!
I didn't do anything wrong, god!

And while you're at it, could you give some money
to Victory Outreach Church? They seem to be doing good things
here. And could you make my man either get really sick
or get better altogether so he'll treat me like a woman for once?
I'm counting on you, god.
And when nice women want to have children
I don't understand why you don't let them. Could you
do something about this? Help the right ones, god—
you should know who they are!

And, god, I'm always blessing everyone in your name.
I hope you don't mind. I do it with a good heart.
But could you help me remember
just one good thing that happened to me as a child?
It's all so dark when I think back, but I know
there must've been something good
because I'm good, really god, I am.

And would you tell those kids in the house
next to mine to stop selling drugs? Please, god,

this is important. There are babies in this neighborhood,
and kids playing in the streets and riding their bicycles,
and I don't want anyone to get hurt, god.

And could you spend a little more time in Barelas?
I think you forget about us down here sometimes, god.
We are good. We want you to pay attention to us,
especially my friends who sleep on the lawn at the
Coronado elementary school on Fourth. We talk to you all the time.

Aren't you listening?

Gladiola

The beauty of the hot pink gladiola
is almost too much
to bear—its color like swelled lips,
lips that have kissed too much.
The arc of its stalk curves
as if it's the hand of a dancer, reaching
up toward an imagined sky, the uppermost flowers
not yet opened.
Their fragrance, anyway, is slight,
and for all their color, they feel unpainted,
yet generous, like the love of a ten-year-old girl,
before makeup and puberty.

I like looking up
at this flower, purchased today at Wild Oats
for exactly $1.59 with the thought of buying
a good deal of beauty at a tiny price.
And, it's true, the slant of the stalk
could set me to dancing—it's Saturday night,
after all, and the buffalo grass is growing,
the laundry's drying on the metal wire
in the backyard, and the moon is only half-full
or half-empty, depending on the tilt
of your thoughts as you dare to look up
into the city sky with its desperate and yearning stars
just dying to show their light.

The Painted and the Real

The datura in his painting
is not the datura with its sweet,
rich scent hovering over the kitchen table,
though they might look alike
in exacting ways, the white flute
of the two flowers plays different music.

His name is the same as so many men—
uncle, mother's high school sweetheart, ex-lovers.
And yet when I say his name it is new every time,
this air breathing life into its syllables,
ripening the fruit of what's common.

I remember the cherries on the tree in Jacona.
My landlady cried when I left that house,
the ditch running right through the yard,
walks in the *barrancas* made of dust,
sudden paths emerging as my feet planted slowly.

At Hotevilla waiting for the butterfly dance to begin,
we wandered dirt roads soft with longing, sweet with rain.
In the empty-chaired plaza, clearing and preparation,
Hopis passing by as we sat separately watchful.
A butterfly, golden in the early morning light, appeared over my head,
hovered there too briefly to tell.
Later that morning the dancers wore tablitas painted with butterflies.
The real evoked the dance.
Or did the dance evoke what's real?

Already he speaks: *I love you* and I ask
how do you know? I am not rebuking him,
only curious for the ways in which these words
are said or not said, for the difference they make.
I love you opens me as the crooked sting of lightning opened the sky
in Los Alamos this week, after the rain that blinded us.

Believe me, I want to see everything.
I want, once again, to ask for everything.
This means lovemaking on the grass
behind adobe wall in rain,
later hearing impatience in his voice
over phone wire, then faith that this larger canvas
will find its place on these walls.

Today he said he wants to be the only one.
My heart is a letter bomb: all it'll take is the ripping
open of the envelope to set it off. It follows
the Rio Grande from Lama to the south valley of Albuquerque,
rich with death and singing, like the earth in this yard,
and how digging down into it, I come quickly to water.

The Storm That Tames Us

We must do more than look
at the flowers. The gardener's pleasure:
labor and the fruits of labor. The digging
and the careful placing of seeds, the tending, the waiting.
When the green shoot first breaks ground,
it is the sound of birthing we like most.

We must begin. We've loved over continents and cultures
to bring ourselves here, on the road between *barrio* and village,
loving with a yearning toward intelligence,
if intelligence is a kind of fire of the mind.

I have watched you come at me
like watching clouds gather on the far horizon
toward storm. I have watched the storm of you
gather and have felt it in my breasts
like the wet scent of near-rain in the northeast
air of my beginnings, or like smelling sage after rain.

Once, I was in the sky all the way to you, asking:
Is this the territory of my dead?
—endless azure and cotton, the roads
snaking far below. There were lights sparkling
across the distant backdrop of a sprawling city.
I come closer to the buildings that house those lights,
just to see the structure there.

Yes, I'm terrified to begin again, as if beginning
holds already the tenuous seeds of loss, made to break us.

Yet the deads' shadows have circled and embraced us.
I ask myself: What was all that's gone before?
Your hands resonate years of lived desire.
I hear the way the leaves are falling.

I have said yes to the question of union.
I've watched you crawl under the colors
of your death-blanket and didn't turn away.
On Xmas, we came through the church door
at Taos Pueblo, from inner dark to the night's dark,
stunning with fire.

I stood in the courtyard looking under the wooden lintel,
through the doorway into more dark, into the white canopy
held over the queen's head, into the wind lifting
the canopy and, beyond, the smoked sky and air
shot the color of pomegranate. The open door,
and again, the white canopy lifting.

We walk the earth with something like intent
circling our days, leave with something more than intent
taking us away. Do we know the seeds of our dying?
You are the vehicle of my return
to this place of silence where objects begin
to live again. Where your eyes save me.

Last summer, at someone else's wedding, I rose up
out of the crowd of single women, as if lifting an arm
to light a torch I could barely reach. I grabbed
that bouquet out of thin mountain air, out of the grips
of another woman, knowing in my blood I am next.
It was a move of pure instinct, born of waiting.

Labor and the fruits of labor.
Days all you get is the digging.
Days all you get is the fruit.
This storm has arrived to tame us. All these years
the air heavy with it and we knew nothing else.
Now we get the release. At last we get the release.

The Beginning Island

Surrender and celebration in equal measure, we married at *Tanah Barak* to the sound of water falling and Sanskrit on the Hindu priest's lips, faces smiling at us in two languages.

This island, both vast and enclosed, where the scent of nasturtium rose from the edges of rice fields into our bed. Out the window, the half-hidden volcano, a fragment of plenty, like what remains of Sappho.

The second ceremony, in Gloucester on the Atlantic, pulled by family history and seaweed back to childhood when things happened easily. We married in Olson's town, in a circle bordered by rocks, filled with morning light, showing only the way in.

In the round, green spotted rock wet with sea, I felt the sea's breath, its waves and light, the surf's pounding in the palm of my hand, in my skin and heart, like a prayer or a song, the rock's hardness growing in me like someone else's life, mixed with the ancient sweetness of Italian honey, my father-in-law and grandmother dancing.

A friend writes: *marriage is moving to another country, a different way of being, another language, another basis of meaning.*

I dismantled the singleness of my life, the solitude as I'd known it, breaking up and redefining what I'd named as my own.

Out of sheer repetition of vows and ceremony, we married—ritual arithmetic of knowing each other, the ways we are written together now.

Rites

Cold marks our breath
I chase sun to the riverbank
Your fire soothes this dark

Mountainair dining:
I face in, you face out
This is how our eyes meet

At nine months, the birth
of a marriage—his room, her room,
the same under stars.

my husband slicing
chives over baked potatoes—I cry,
suddenly everything's lit from within.

Your bare hand
holding space between us
I match you finger for finger

You, my husband, are
the reason I can look straight
into other men's eyes.

Leaving the Fields of Hydrangeas

I have said yes because I like the sound.
We arrive at a field made blue by hydrangea.
I've never known the meaning of enough.

Women and children's voices are deliberate and round.
Gamelan, the music of spells, scent of clove-spice—
I have said yes because I like the sound.

Full moon's rising over *kecak's* fire and chant,
what's magic is allowed to come alive.
I've never known the meaning of enough.

Women sing hello like my grandmother's round
of song, dress me, pat my butt, say *bagus*.
I have said yes because I like the sound.

Double ikat cloth, endless good from the gods,
Sapphire and gold, underwater blue, blue of his eyes—
I've never known the meaning of enough.

What's real is more of a dream than the dream.
The dance outside the dance outside the dance.
I have said yes because I like the sound.
I'll never know the meaning of enough.

The Splitting of the Domestic

1

When a woman cries
it is the earth that most needs
her tears. The once-swollen river
now full of dust. The mountains,
asking, asking for snow.

When a woman cries
she wakes up her mate; her children
rub their eyes with the crooks
of their fingers. Everyone watching,
watching the way the road curves.

And why is she crying

2

It is a fascination
for what's deep:
sleeping out of doors
under ceiling of cloud and star
staring into sky like swimming in a dark sea

and asking, asking all
she'd never found answers for:
what is matter

can objects hold intent
do feet planted in earth bring what's hidden there to form

and anyway, what zone is this somewhere between
heaven and earth

3

She opens the dictionary
to words she needs
to know the meaning of:
red   fecundity

Maybe lodged somewhere
in the center of that stone
she's saved for years now
is the image of a man walking
a faraway beach   and bending

It is like in dreams when you go home
but don't know where you are

4

Yes, water keeps things alive—
and the land, dry or after a hard rain,
gives our spirit back to us. Einstein said:
matter is energy reduced to the point of visibility.
She encloses the stone in her palm.

And that stone holds what the heart held
behind the hand that bent to pick it up
all those years ago. Time is irrelevant
when it comes to the heart,
which when allowed to open, does.

her tears nourish like rain
her tears fill the air with questions
her tears make even the desert fecund

water rushes by the metal gate,
free at last to go its course, to go where it's needed
filling fields, horses' mouths, gardens and ditches,
contained and directed, and flowing:

where there's lack there's a need to gather and save.

The Fire Notebooks

SINGLENESS

Doesn't every woman long to be seductress—deep slit in the black dress, French perfume, unrevealed spot in the private woods by the lake, the place from which there is no need of names? Perhaps I exaggerate the romance. There is more to it, or less: hotel room under heat of noonday sun, nothing to do with love that lasts but rather with the speed of light in a darkened room, with hands and breath—fields of the possible.

A woman alone at the end of the twentieth century knows how to be taken by the sense of wanting another, yet also rooted there. She knows the grace of the temporary. A breaking of form, convention, an opening, an awakening—the way Kerouac wrote *On the Road* on a roll of teletype paper because he didn't want to stop his flow of words to change the sheet of paper. The world goes by that quickly if we're willing to get on.

Always after a particular and elusive brand of *tough*—if only the black leather bike jacket with its steel zippers would fit, then it would be clear how to release all kinds of love with eyes of scrutiny and delight, the single woman's tools. When we dare to remember the glow on the tail of the comet, still cloaked under the dark of night, we'd dare to remember every such love, why there are those who come to us to show us we'd do anything for them.

Goodbye, single woman I have walked with to the edge of night. In the face of marriage, my hope is your survival.

STRONGHOLD

The house had its own rhythm that I came to know as I would come to know a lover, with both hands reaching out, out, and all of me singing. I moved to Barelas, the house offered to me, a papaya split open on a bright blue plate. That ripe orange fruit was a gift waiting to be raised to the lips and eaten. So I ate and slept and woke breathing the rarefied air of solitude—that refuge, that stronghold, that place without witnesses.

On Halloween, dozens and dozens of kids appeared on my doorstep, costumed and smiling, holding out their empty candy bags to be filled, to be filled. I was in that neighborhood, but not of it, wondering what there was to see among trash, crooked fences, dark boys driving their low-slung cars. It broke my heart and opened it at once, that dark beauty.

In my home, I planted bulbs and landscaped with scalloped brick and gathered stone. Police cars emerged hard and fast from nowhere, sped down Santa Fe Avenue with sirens blasting. I sunk my feet into an untended earth, turned it so it, too, could breathe. That house, once abandoned, now mostly filled with light. On the front porch, little Danielle sang a song about angels, the air crisp with fall, the house holding itself steady on the earth.

THE FIRE

I married and left that house to fend for itself. Another walked its floors, slept in its rooms. Even so, my heart lingered, echoing in vacancy. Then fire ate all of it, till the skin on my palms turned grey. This ashen breath of home. Place from which I claimed my place on earth, now black. Shock of obliteration, transformation—even in bright daylight every room is dark. It is impossible to see how I once moved here, how I once named this home.

I entered solitude as if it were a gift I earned after so many years of gathering others about myself—gift of bleached bone. The desert sun reveals all—woman alone at twentieth century's end embracing an untaught way of being. Before one comes to live in solitude, one comes to loneliness. But how deep the breath is there, finally the nourishing quality of air. And who has not displaced herself to find the way home?

Burn away the emotion of being alone on the earth. Burn away the idea that this gift cannot be carried within. Burn away the last unclean element of disbelief. The past is obliterated, the space cleared. A beautiful space I no longer occupy, gleaming with light.

THE NEW FORM

Marriage allows us to have a witness to the mundane, a chain of days of immediacy, an attentiveness to the way the flowers bloom and die, especially the datura whose shape is most known after dark, whose fragrance overwhelms until the flower's cut from its root, quickly dispersing its scent. I marry to continue the business of cultivating a self, to find solitude with a new background that includes the sounds of one other.

Before I had solitude and an intimate relationship with space. Now I have solitude and communion with another. And I still want the other like the need for salt in the tropics, skin shining with heat and moisture, sweat beading on the back of neck, under the straw of hat, when thirst is unquenchable and the need for salt acute, the way our hungers shift in shifting climates.

This ground gives me new daring, every day the words: *I need to face what I love.* Not obsessively, but with necessary abandon, in a dimension of peacefulness. Walking down roads we haven't been on, immersing ourselves in the language of others. Now when I say *husband*, the word washes over me, soothes me. And I was so afraid. Fear: the necessary element in becoming.

What lasts takes its deserved seat beside me. I join hands with all that has given me shape, open the window, let our voices mix in the wind.

The Rhythm of Chance

Is it chance or readiness, the moment when fire decides to catch and all the smoking wood takes deliciously to flame? There's something to the preparation—each stick of kindling perfectly balanced, resting against each other as if they could stay that way…then the disappointment when they fall into themselves, seeming to give up. Yet we are warmed by such fire.

Incalculable. Lucky. So many years of trying on other lives, only to find they don't fit. And is it luck to turn toward one you've known as friend, suddenly see the silk in his shirt as seductive? Will the stories we've told each other lead us finally toward home?

And the point is this: not to give the self away. I write in a room whose door I can shut. As the latch clicks wordlessly into place, every life I've lived breathes again. This is as alone as I would want to be. The more I spin and turn in this space I slowly name my own, the more the seductress lives, or the little girl, or the woman who doesn't want to be called wife, but is, or the lover, or the ex-con or the French woman at the turn of the previous century, finding her way home.

I would not want it otherwise in this clear and tossed light.

Leaving a Trace

Winter approaches:
indecisive steed, white field.
I contemplate struc-
ture, all the seasons of wild
intent, place stone atop stone.

He writes of becoming
an old-aged poet—last time
he wrote "middle-aged"...
thinking of him, the ageless sky
opens to a rare, desert rain.

Calling my name across
bleachers—his existential
wail haunted me
for the rest of the weekend
through the sweet breath of husband

Its pink lips open
in layers like fireworks
coolly delicate
pure white stalk underneath—
lone blossom on the Christmas cactus.

As a boy, he buried
crystals in the roots of a lemon tree.
As a man, he returns to unearth
the stones, places them on his desk—
Can the past protect us this way?

toasted hazelnuts
cracked open by the wood-fire
I fill his bowl
with their empty husks
as he drives away

A bird's breast, her tool.
She makes nests with her entire body,
heart repeatedly
pressing against scraps, twigs—
the gathered, raw material.

waking slowly
I place my hand on his face
all around us, air
turns from fall to winter:
our breath begins to leave a trace.

Legacy

It's what's in the distance that matters—
grey skyline across abundant Charles,
the North End of Boston
where the lady who owns the religious articles store laments:
this *used to be* an Italian neighborhood.

Last night I dreamt of giving birth
to a girl, my daughter, I said,
and no longer felt I didn't belong in this world.
But I didn't know how to care for her,
how to move down the street holding her hand.

When I talk to my grandmother, who's ninety-two,
I hear the song in her voice that is rich with welcome and delight.
I do not hear the sound of her crochet needles echo
through rooms of longing and absence, or the sound
of my dead grandfather's voice repeating itself in her head.

This year Mother Teresa died. And my husband's father.
Now Allen Ginsberg and Bill can shake each other's eternal hands.
With each public or private death we question
our own place on earth, in outrage or sadness,
watch the world spin on.

And here we are, making love on a new mattress,
when so many can't speak to each other,
as our dead spin away from us into their own new worlds,
and we eat, we drink, we carry on with this legacy,
past sifting into present, our hands tied and reaching out, at once.

Ghazal for October's End

My pen ran out of ink.
That doesn't mean I have nothing left to say.

This morning even the telephone wire is free
of birds, whose feet usually discern voice.

Last night her voice, subdued and quieter than it's been,
reached me with its sad, familiar pulse.

Did you know before blood comes a woman often walks,
like a mountain lion, the abyss of what she hunts or most needs?

Released from a system that was once support,
she sees the many ways of her depletion.

That with a woman's blood there is elation or disappointment—
every month not a thing taken for granted.

Hundreds of red chiles dry on house walls at Jemez.
We search for hot pools to immerse our bodies in.

By the river the cottonwood leaves have shifted to gold.
A heron's blue wings cut through autumn's clear air.

Pulling Vinca

The vinca, planted long before
I arrived, in the wrong sheltered
places, has taken hold, roots trailing
just under the earth's surface, choking everything
else that tries to live, like fighter planes
weaving in and out of each other trail smoke
in an otherwise unparanoid sky

*If you had known me
once, you'd still know me now**

A trailing habit,
the Western Garden Book says,
so although we pull it up,
everywhere, its roots spread;
everywhere, it asks for more.

But we don't want to give it
more, no need here to encourage
its wantonness, its shameless desire
to always go where it pleases, to be
all over the place, to be the only one.

So, despite ourselves, we pull
the long tangled masses of roots
until they come free of the earth
that binds them, cart them completely
out of the yard so they won't surreptitiously
take root again without our noticing.

We want peace here, after all!
—yellow tulips with red stripes
that claim the insides of their skins,
multicolored pansies and bright marigolds,
orange poppies and an occasional blue anemone,
flowers we transplant but can't yet name.

We want it all—yes, I suppose,
even the vinca that invisibly spreads its root system—
everything must be allowed to grow
in this yard now mixed with your sweat
and mine, in this place no one has ever known
us by, though we are who we've always been,
just newly aligned, moving differently because of it.

*Adrienne Rich:
"Atlas of the Difficult World"

Fragile Quartet

1

I have wanted to go toward what I was afraid of—

deep ravine in the thick heat of Bali
gut wrenching crossing,
fear beginning at center, then spreading

like one drop of blackberry
on the white porcelain sink
like blood in the fibers of a shirt

Then I remembered the fragility in the bones of my mother

2

This making and breaking of words
this making of a home
I can fully inhabit

Unearthing boxes unopened for ten years,
so much flowing out,
and with those pieces of paper, pieces of heart

3

Over the Sandias, clouds as towers
of moisture and light. I have flown
through thunderheads to meet my husband
down here on an earth clarified by rain,
a grace that washes out what's past

Words emerge at a deep level of form,
invisible and trustworthy as old love letters
in boxes: Can we live with who we've been?

4

Passion determines shape.
In marriage we mix objects
as much as ideas, our house built
from the heart outward, toward habitat

Planes can drop thousands of feet in a second—
how brief our time on earth,

how easily our bones break,
how hard to find wings and hearth
in our two breaths.

Whatever Is

Not the luster of ruby,
but the carbon imperfection.

Not the sea,
but the sea's dead bounty.

Not the sanctuary of cathedral,
but the old woman mopping its floors.

Not the grey flesh of the dying,
but their far-reaching advice.

Not the fury of lovemaking,
but the sweet drunk sky.

Not the 14,000-foot summit,
but the breath finding origin.

Not his death after the operation,
but the hour of laughter he orchestrated before.

Not the garden's yield,
but each day's watering.

Not the wedding parties,
but the dents in the pillows their heads make.

Not the stark sun at noon,
but the sharp shadows.

Not the parents holding on,
but the child's first raucous steps.

Not that it should not be,
but that it is.

Returning to Center

I heard a pueblo woman say
in the Southwest,
when you go outside,
skies so broad and deep,
a huge circle surrounds you.
You are the exact center,
and community is more
than just what's human.

But can I take the center
with me, say in Manhattan or London,
in a swirl of faces and buildings,
where so often it is impossible
to see out?

Driving Route 50,
the "loneliest highway in America",
the Lazy B and Salt Wells whorehouses shut tight,
petroglyphs on volcanic rock
under skies rich with black clouds and air force testing planes,
a lone woman with a flag stops traffic.
Suddenly there is a line of cars
because she's done so,
and the center narrows.

We receive a note from a friend:
dear fellow capitalists, he writes—
these are days when Morningstar
is a company whose advice we seek,
not a light we look up to as we wake.

wenty years ago a palm reader
in Burma said he'd get prostate cancer
in his fifty-third year
so, all that year
he cancels each appointment
he's made with a doctor

we lay in the rain
on a lawn in Glorieta,
our clothes strewn on the edges
of blanket, skin tasting each slow
drop of water. Later, we wrote quick poems
on the white refrigerator out of
magnetized letters:
you wrote: eat hot petal whisper/skin chant moan.
I wrote: I did always what I would with you,
blue frantic blood.

No, I don't want to be fooled
by anything anymore. Starting now,
my eyes will be as open as the doors
at Indian gaming halls.

Some men understand
that when a woman opens
her legs to them
she opens her soul.
Most don't.

I take a hot bath,
watch shadows form on the stucco
of the house next door, listen to
my dark neighbor's rake
grating the hard earth,
sounds of Saturday night cruising,
Spanish songs blaring briefly and loudly,
reminding me oddly of Paris' left bank,
all that life in the streets.

Homeboys don't look you in the eyes
when you run by them. They stand still,
hands in pants' pockets, stare straight
in front of themselves. I know they see me.
After I pass, I hear the inevitable whistle,
a sharp sound, brittle as train whistle.
It makes me laugh as I run in my black baggy sweats,
red socks inside purple and ochre Nikes,
obviously not caring how I look.
Yet how invincible I feel. I carry my keys
like mace gripped in my hands, hidden,
down Eighth to Silver and west all the way
to the catalpa trees on Thirteenth,
odd and twisted like knuckles. I
smile when I'm under their hands,
like being under wings.

Goddess, help me be strong
and tender and forthright and supple,
will you?
I lived in that house
redone by Mario's hands,
a house nearly abandoned,
inhabited by junkies and mad dogs
chained to the toilet,
a house where weeds
covered the doorways. Yes,
I lived there, in a house
whose foundation
is volcanic rock,
near a woman who lay seized up
in her front yard while the paramedics came,
asking all the wrong questions,
her shirtsleeves hugging her wrists,
and while they worked on her,
a man with his clothes in a bag
left out the back door, glancing sideways—
all this on a Sunday walk
to the river in summer.

Coor's Road, Albuquerque,
a sign reads:
coldest ice in town.

Days no matter where I go,
the Southwest, foreign cities,
the enclosing bay of San Francisco,
inside or out, I carry the circle
within, and the center simply holds.

On the rabbit hunt,
following close behind the hunter
with his bows and arrows,
I wondered what I'd do
if he actually killed one,
fresh death in our hands.
I thought of the daughter
who died in a car wreck
whose father received a transplant
of her heart into his body.
He lives on, heart-broken,
preferring the heart to be
beating in her body.

That afternoon he smeared blood
across the face of my belly,
pulled it out of me with outstretched fingers.
My blood surrounded him then,
dried on his hands, shifting color
as leaves do at the change of season.
A precious hunt.

Mother Teresa said
none of us can do great things,
but we can do small things
with great love.

Explaining his past, he said:
You have to look at this
altar boy stuff as my first
introduction into magic,

the repetition of sacred words—
a language I didn't know
the meaning of. I totally
enjoyed the sound.

The air hot
with oil and spinning food,
he tosses the mushrooms
over a high blue flame.
They roll over one another
like waves. He says: come here,
smell this. His face
is a hot blue flame.
The kitchen smells of Italy and Japan.
Everything's on high.
He refuses a spatula,
tests meat with the tips of his fingers.

Good Friday.
No longer the good Catholic girl.
No longer church on Sundays,
mortal and venial sins, or
the priest's disembodied voice
in the confessional.

Cry me a river,
he used to say
when I complained
about love.
Yesterday's ultrasound,

wand of camera running
back and forth over belly
to view what seemed
the darkest sea on earth.
Entire belly became sea
and the dark, dense spots
rising in that sea, the unknown.
Photographs of cervix, ovaries,
walls of uterus and the long canal
to that place made of sex, which, after all,
is a kind of birthing.

Listen to the wood and how it sings,
he writes,
the moment of its splitting.

I've been listening so long
to the sound of splitting;
now I want to know
the sound wood makes when it's whole.

Colophon

Set in ADOBE GARAMOND—
a version of the French Renaissance face
by Claude Garamond/Robert Granjon
distinguished by an x-height pared toward
refined density and graceful intimacy.
Designed by Robert Slimbach *(1988)*.

Titling is Post Mediæval.
Designed by Herbert Post *(1932-35)*.
•

Book design by J. Bryan

Renée Gregorio, originally from Massachusetts, has lived in New Mexico since 1985. She was one of the founding editors of *The Taos Review* and one of the featured writers in the video, *Honoring the Muse*. Her work has appeared in literary journals in both the United States and England as well as in several anthologies of poetry, including *The New Mexico Poetry Renaissance* and *Saludos!*. Several chapbooks of her poems have been published by Yoo-Hoo Press of Farmington, New Mexico, X Press of Santa Fe, and Twelfth Street Press of Providence, Rhode Island. Gregorio is a former member of the jazz/poetry group, Luminous Animal, and has read her work throughout the Southwest and performed in Dead Poets' bouts, and won. She earned her master's degree from Antioch University, London. Her first full-length collection, *The Skins of Possible Lives*, was published by Blinking Yellow Books of Taos, New Mexico in 1996. She and her husband, John Brandi, make their home in Corrales.